Tools

Search
Notes

Discuss
MyReportLinks.com Books
Go!

STATES

WASHINGTON

A MyReportLinks.com Book

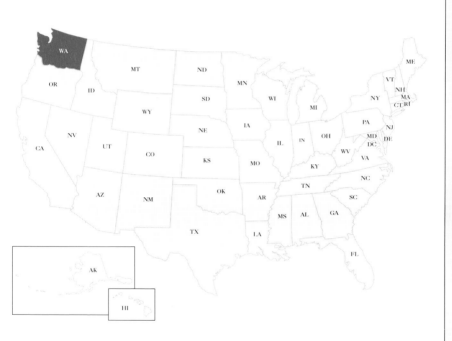

Stephen Feinstein

MyReportLinks.com Books

an imprint of

Enslow Publishers, Inc.

Box 398, 40 Industrial Road

Berkeley Heights, NJ 07922

USA

MyReportLinks.com Books, an imprint of Enslow Publishers, Inc. MyReportLinks is
a trademark of Enslow Publishers, Inc.

Library of Congress Cataloging-in-Publication Data

Feinstein, Stephen.
  Washington / Stephen Feinstein.
      p. cm. — (States)
  Summary: Discusses the land and climate, economy, govern-
ment, and history of the forty-second state to join the Union.
Includes Internet links to Web sites, source documents, and
photographs related to Washington.
  Includes bibliographical references and index.
  ISBN 0-7660-5026-2
  1. Washington (State)—Juvenile literature. [1. Washington
(State)] I. Title. II. Series: States (Series : Berkeley
Heights, N.J.)
F891.3.F45 2002
979.7—dc21

                       2002008692

Printed in the United States of America

10 9 8 7 6 5 4 3 2 1

To Our Readers:
Through the purchase of this book, you and your library gain access to the Report Links that specifically back
up this book.
The Publisher will provide access to the Report Links that back up this book and will keep these Report Links
up to date on **www.myreportlinks.com** for three years from the book's first publication date.
We have done our best to make sure all Internet addresses in this book were active and appropriate when we
went to press. However, the author and the Publisher have no control over, and assume no liability for, the
material available on those Internet sites or on other Web sites they may link to.
The usage of the MyReportLinks.com Books Web site is subject to the terms and conditions stated on the
Usage Policy Statement on **www.myreportlinks.com**.
In the future, a password may be required to access the Report Links that back up this book. The password
is found on the bottom of page 4 of this book.
Any comments or suggestions can be sent by e-mail to comments@myreportlinks.com or to the address on
the back cover.

Photo Credits: America's Story from America's Library/Library of Congress, p. 15; © Corel
Corporation, pp. 3, 10, 23, 26, 31; © 1995 PhotoDisc, pp. 30, 32; © 1999 PhotoDisc, pp. 20,
33, 45; © Corbis Corp. American Destinations, p. 24; Enslow Publishers, Inc., pp. 1, 19;
MyReportLinks.com Books, p. 4; National Park Service, pp. 38, 43; Official Site of Washington State
Tourism, Office of Trade and Economic Development, pp. 12, 22; PBS/Lewis and Clark, p. 40;
Salon.com, p. 17; Salmon Recovery Home Page, p. 28; Space Needle, p. 13; State of Washington,
p. 35; *The Detroit News*, p. 18.

Cover Photo: © Corbis Corporation, American Destinations.

Cover Description: Mount Rainier

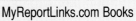
Contents

Back	Forward	Stop	Review	Home	Explore	Favorites	History

About MyReportLinks.com Books

MyReportLinks.com Books
Great Books, Great Links, Great for Research!

MyReportLinks.com Books present the information you need to learn about your report subject. In addition, they show you where to go on the Internet for more information. The pre-evaluated Report Links that back up this book are kept up to date on **www.myreportlinks.com**. With the purchase of a MyReportLinks.com Books title, you and your library gain access to the Report Links that specifically back up that book. The Report Links save hours of research time and link to dozens—even hundreds—of Web sites, source documents, and photos related to your report topic.

Please see "To Our Readers" on the Copyright page for important information about this book, the MyReportLinks.com Books Web site, and the Report Links that back up this book.

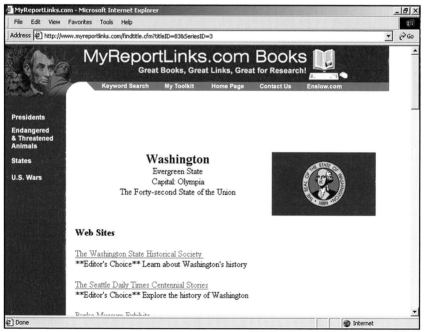

Access:

The Publisher will provide access to the Report Links that back up this book and will try to keep these Report Links up to date on our Web site for three years from the book's first publication date. Please enter **SWA3713** if asked for a password.

Report Links

 The Internet sites described below can be accessed at
http://www.myreportlinks.com

*EDITOR'S CHOICE

▶ **The Washington State Historical Society**
At the Washington State Historical Society Web site you will find four
online exhibits which explore Washington's history. You will also find a
historic time line and links to additional resources about Washington.

Link to this Internet site from http://www.myreportlinks.com

*EDITOR'S CHOICE

▶ **The *Seattle Daily Times* Centennial Stories**
At the *Seattle Daily Times* Web site, you will find articles, photographs, and
study guides describing over one hundred years of northwestern history.

Link to this Internet site from http://www.myreportlinks.com

*EDITOR'S CHOICE

▶ **Burke Museum Exhibits**
At the Burke Museum of Natural History and Culture, you can explore
many online exhibits. Here you will find exhibits about earthquakes in
the Pacific Northwest, mammals in Washington, the Kennewick man,
and other interesting exhibits.

Link to this Internet site from http://www.myreportlinks.com

*EDITOR'S CHOICE

▶ **Explore the States: Washington**
America's Story from America's Library, a Library of Congress Web site
provides a brief overview of basic facts about Washington. You will also
find links to more information about Washington.

Link to this Internet site from http://www.myreportlinks.com

*EDITOR'S CHOICE

▶ **Access Washington: State Facts**
At this Web site you will find facts about Washington's population,
state government, history, geography, economics, and much more.

Link to this Internet site from http://www.myreportlinks.com

*EDITOR'S CHOICE

▶ **Lewis and Clark**
Here you will find maps, time lines, journal entries, and articles
chronicling Lewis and Clark's expedition. You can also read about the
inner-workings of the Corps of Discovery.

Link to this Internet site from http://www.myreportlinks.com

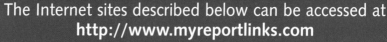

 The Internet sites described below can be accessed at
http://www.myreportlinks.com

▶ **Century 21—The 1962 Seattle World's Fair**
At this Web site you can read an essay about Century 21, the 1962 World's Fair. You will also find images of posters, magazine covers, and photographs of the fair, including the Space Needle and the monorail.

Link to this Internet site from http://www.myreportlinks.com

▶ **Earthquake Processes: Cascadia Subduction Zone**
Here you will find technical descriptions, diagrams, and maps illustrating the collision of the Juan de Fuca and North American tectonic plates. You will also learn how this process results in earthquakes.

Link to this Internet site from http://www.myreportlinks.com

▶ **Experience Music Project**
The home of the Experience Music Project museum in Seattle contains items related to Jimi Hendrix. You will also find a vast collection of feature articles, interviews, photographs, video files, and sound files.

Link to this Internet site from http://www.myreportlinks.com

▶ **Experience Washington**
At the official Washington State Tourism Web site, you will find dozens of beautiful photographs and descriptions of places to visit in Washington.

Link to this Internet site from http://www.myreportlinks.com

▶ **Gary Larson**
At this Web site you can read an article about the life and work of *The Far Side* creator and Seattle native Gary Larson.

Link to this Internet site from http://www.myreportlinks.com

▶ **Governor Gary Locke**
At the official State of Washington Web site you can read the biography of Governor Gary Locke, learn about his policies, and read his speeches. You can also take a virtual tour of the Executive Mansion.

Link to this Internet site from http://www.myreportlinks.com

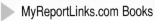
Report Links

 The Internet sites described below can be accessed at
http://www.myreportlinks.com

▶ **Jimi Hendrix Experience**
At the Rock and Roll Hall of Fame Web site you will find a brief
biography and time line of one of popular music's greatest innovators,
Washington native Jimi Hendrix.

Link to this Internet site from http://www.myreportlinks.com

▶ **Klondike Gold Rush—Seattle Unit**
The National Park Service Web site provides a brief history of the
Klondike Gold Rush in Seattle. You will also find links to
comprehensive histories of the Klondike Gold Rush.

Link to this Internet site from http://www.myreportlinks.com

▶ **Kurt Cobain and a dream about pop**
At this Web site you can read an article about Kurt Cobain, a native
Washingtonian. Here you will learn about Cobain's life and the impact
his band, Nirvana, had on music.

Link to this Internet site from http://www.myreportlinks.com

▶ **Minoru Yamasaki, world-class architect**
At this Web site you will find a biography of Seattle native, Japanese-
American architect Minoru Yamasaki. You will also find photographs
of Yamasaki and some of his most noteworthy buildings.

Link to this Internet site from http://www.myreportlinks.com

▶ **Mount Rainier National Park**
At the National Park Service Web site, you will learn about the United
States' fifth largest peak, Mount Rainier. Here you will find photographs
and facts about volcanic activity.

Link to this Internet site from http://www.myreportlinks.com

▶ **Mount St. Helens, Washington**
The United States Geological Survey Web site provides a history of Mount
Saint Helens eruptions, up-to-date monitoring of volcanic activity, articles,
photographs, maps, and other Mount Saint Helens resources.

Link to this Internet site from http://www.myreportlinks.com

 The Internet sites described below can be accessed at
http://www.myreportlinks.com

▶ **North West Company**
At this Web site you will learn about the North West Company, a fur-trading company from the eighteenth and nineteenth century that was situated in part of what is now Oregon.

Link to this Internet site from http://www.myreportlinks.com

▶ **Olympic National Park**
At the National Park Service Web site you can explore the Olympic National Park's forests, seashore, mountains, rivers, and people. You will also learn about the wildlife, endangered species, and ecosystem management.

Link to this Internet site from http://www.myreportlinks.com

▶ **Quincy Jones: The Story of an American Musician**
At the PBS Web site you will find a comprehensive essay about musician, songwriter, producer, and arranger, Quincy Jones. Learn about his life as a boy growing up in Seattle.

Link to this Internet site from http://www.myreportlinks.com

▶ **Salmon Recovery Home Page**
Here you will find news, statistics, legislation, and other items related to Washington's salmon recovery effort. Learn how you can get involved.

Link to this Internet site from http://www.myreportlinks.com

▶ **Space Needle**
At the official Web site of the Space Needle, you will find history, trivia, an online tour, tourist information, and everything else you have always wanted to know about of Seattle's most famous landmark.

Link to this Internet site from http://www.myreportlinks.com

▶ **Stately Knowledge: Washington**
At this Web site you will find facts and figures about the state of Washington. You will also find links to other Internet resources.

Link to this Internet site from http://www.myreportlinks.com

Report Links

The Internet sites described below can be accessed at
http://www.myreportlinks.com

▶ **The Symbols of Washington State**
At this Web site you will find pictures and descriptions of Washington's
state symbols. Also included are the lyrics to the state song and the state
folk song.

Link to this Internet site from http://www.myreportlinks.com

▶ **Theodore Roethke (1908–1963)**
Here you will find poems by Theodore Roethke and a biography that
discusses his life and poetry. You will also learn about his career as an
educator at the University of Washington and other schools.

Link to this Internet site from http://www.myreportlinks.com

▶ **U.S. Census Bureau: Washington**
At this Web site you will find the official census statistics on the state
of Washington. Learn about the population figures, business facts,
geography facts, and more.

Link to this Internet site from http://www.myreportlinks.com

▶ **Washington: A Little Trip to the Extraordinary**
At this Web site you will find a listing of information about
Washington, including topography, maps, weather, state flower,
and much more.

Link to this Internet site from http://www.myreportlinks.com

▶ **Washington Native American Tribes**
At this Web site you can link to the online homes of Washington's
American Indian tribes, from the Chehalis to the Upper Skagit.

Link to this Internet site from http://www.myreportlinks.com

▶ **William Henry Gates, III**
This biography on Bill Gates by ABC News provides a brief overview
of the famous entrepreneur's life and links to recent articles about the
multibillionaire and his corporation, Microsoft.

Link to this Internet site from http://www.myreportlinks.com

Washington Facts

Capital
Olympia

Population
5,894,121*

Gained Statehood
November 11, 1889;
the forty-second state

Bird
Willow goldfinch (also
known as the wild canary)

Tree
Western hemlock

Flower
Coast (or western)
rhododendron

Fish
Steelhead trout

Insect
Green darner dragonfly

Fossil
Columbian mammoth

Gem
Petrified wood

Fruit
Apple

Grass
Bluebunch wheatgrass

Dance
Square dance

Ship
President Washington

Song
"Washington, My Home"
(written by Helen Davis,
arranged by Stuart Churchill)

Flag
The flag's green background
represents the state's forests.
The state seal appears in the
middle. It includes a portrait
of George Washington, and
the words "The Seal of the
State of Washington 1889."

Motto
Al-ki (an American Indian
word meaning "bye and bye")

Nickname
Evergreen State

*Population reflects the 2000 census.

Chapter 1 ▶

The Evergreen State

Washington, in the northwestern corner of the United States, is a place of startling contrasts. The mighty Cascade Mountains roughly divide the state in half, creating two totally different worlds. These huge volcanic peaks run from Washington's northern border with Canada to its southern border with Oregon.

West of the Cascades, Washington is cool, damp, and green. Most of Washington's nearly 6 million people live here, near or along the shores of Puget Sound. Outside the cities, there are thick evergreen forests along the coasts and on the lower slopes of the mountains.

East of the Cascades, Washington is so dry that certain areas can be considered a desert. A region of gently rolling hills known as the Columbia Plateau makes up much of eastern Washington. Irrigation projects have turned huge areas of these rolling hills and dry grasslands into golden fields of wheat.

▶ Immense Forests

Washington gets its nickname, the Evergreen State, from its immense forests. The forests were important to the American Indians, whose ancestors first settled in coastal areas of what is now Washington at least thirteen thousand years ago. The Snoqualmie, Snohomish, and Nooksack peoples used cedar to make longhouses, wooden structures up to 100 feet long and 40 feet wide. They also made totem poles and carved canoes out of cedar tree trunks.

▲ *Washington is nicknamed the Evergreen State because of its lush, green, rolling hills and vast forests.*

They even made clothing from cedar bark. Lumber is still an important part of Washington's economy.

Washington's forests are part of the beautiful scenery that attracts a large and growing number of tourists each year. Seattle's Space Needle, is a six hundred-foot-tall tower that had been built for the 1962 World's Fair. It offers a magnificent view of the surrounding countryside and waters. On clear days, you can see Mount Rainier, the state's highest mountain at 14,410 feet.

The snow-capped peaks of the Olympic Range rise to the west of Seattle. More than 150 inches of rain fall each year in the river valleys of the Olympic Peninsula. The peninsula is home to the Olympic rain forest in Olympic National Park, the "greenest" part of the Evergreen State. Ferns and moss cover the ground in the rain forest. The evergreen trees are mainly western hemlock, Douglas fir, Sitka spruce, and western red cedar. One writer described standing close to one of these great trees: " . . . to see to the top you must tip back your head until your neck hurts. Trees average two hundred feet high and range to over three hundred feet!"[1] Moss hangs from branches, and water drips constantly from the sky or from the branches overhead. This jungle environment is rare so far north of the tropics.

▲ Built for the 1962 World's Fair, the Space Needle is one of Seattle's most famous landmarks.

▶ Amazing Wildlife

An amazing variety of wildlife inhabits the waters and forests of Washington. Passengers aboard ferryboats in Puget Sound, especially around the San Juan Islands, are likely to see packs, or "pods," of killer whales, known as "orcas." These marine mammals are known to kill and eat seals, otters, dolphins, squid, seabirds, and fish. In Puget Sound, however, they usually only eat fish—mainly salmon, rockfish, and cod. Orcas are very social animals and travel in pods of up to forty individuals. They grow to 32 feet in length, weigh five to six tons, and can travel at more than 30 miles an hour.

During the spring and late fall, migrating California gray whales can be seen along the Pacific coast and sometimes in Puget Sound. The gray whale is a protected species. In 1998, the Makah Indian tribe of northwest Washington was given the right to hunt these whales. Whale hunting used to be an important part of the tribe's lifestyle, but they had been forbidden to hunt the whales for seventy years. Now, the Makah legally can kill up to five whales a year for food. Other species of marine life in Washington's waters include porpoises, seals, and sea lions. The largest species of octopus in the world, which can grow as big as 12 feet across, lives in Puget Sound. Of course, Washington is famous for its salmon.

Washington's land animals include elk, deer, woodland caribou, bighorn sheep, mountain goats, cougars, black bears, and grizzly bears. There are also many varieties of smaller mammals, including beaver, badgers, muskrat, marmots, rabbits, and squirrels. In recent years, small numbers of timber wolves have moved south from British Columbia into Washington's North Cascade and Selkirk mountains.

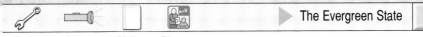

Among the many species of birds in Washington are the spotted owl and the bald eagle. One of Washington's most unusual creatures is the slug, which is basically a snail without its shell. Slugs like western Washington's damp climate, and there are several varieties of slug. Imported European black slugs recently outnumbered the native banana slug.

▶ A Diverse and Creative Population

For many thousands of years, the population of what is now Washington consisted entirely of American Indians. Today they make up less than 2 percent of the state's population. Most Washingtonians—approximately 79

Northwest Folklife Festival - Microsoft Internet Explorer

File   Edit   View   Favorites   Tools   Help

Address 🖻 http://www.americaslibrary.gov/pages/es_wa_whales_1_e.html   ▾ 🔗 Go

Home ★About this site ★Help   The Library of Congress

America's Story from America's Library
Meet Amazing Americans   Jump Back in Time   **Explore the States**   Join America at Play   See, Hear and Sing

Explore the States ▸ Washington

Northwest Folklife Festival   ◀ BACK

The Cape Fox Dancers, 1979 Festival

Credit: "The Cape Fox Dancers, 1979 Festival." Photo by Steve Meltzer, for "Northwest Folklife Festival," a Washington Local Legacies project

🌐 Internet

▲ The Cape Fox dancers, pictured here, are members of the Tlingit tribe in Washington. They perform traditional chants and dances at the annual Northwest Folklife Festival.

percent—are European Americans. Based on the 2000 census, approximately 8 percent of the state's population is Hispanic American, 5 percent Asian American, and 3 percent African American. The percentage of minorities is higher in the larger cities. Seattle elected its first African-American mayor, Norman B. Rice, in 1989. In 1997, Washingtonians elected Gary Locke, the nation's first Chinese-American governor.

Creative people of all kinds, including musicians, writers, and artists, thrive in Washington. A man from Seattle named William Henry "Bill" Gates, III was creative in a different way. At the age of fourteen, he began writing computer programs. In 1975, he started the Microsoft Corporation, which is now one of the nation's biggest companies. Bill Gates has become the richest man in the world.

Rock musician Jimi Hendrix was born in Seattle in 1942. Hendrix, who was part African American, and part American Indian, was an exciting electric guitar player who became an overnight success in 1967. Unfortunately, he died of a drug overdose in 1970. Thirty years later, a museum called the Experience Music Project (EMP) opened in Seattle. Designed by architect Frank Gehry, the EMP features exhibits about Jimi Hendrix and the history of rock 'n' roll.

While Hendrix was still a baby, another great musician—the legendary Ray Charles—was performing in clubs in Seattle. The blind rhythm-and-blues singer met Quincy Jones and formed a band. Jones later became a famous music producer.

Seattle continues to be famous for its musicians and style. The 1980s grunge look—baggy clothes, torn jeans, and combat boots—started in Seattle. Late twentieth century groups from Seattle included Nirvana and Pearl Jam.

Many other creative people were either born in Washington or chose to live there. Robert Joffrey, the dancer and choreographer who founded the world-famous Joffrey Ballet, was born in Seattle and trained to be a dancer there. Washington poets include Carolyn Kizer of Spokane and Theodore Roethke, the "Poet of Puget Sound." Roethke moved to Washington after World War II. His poetry was inspired by the beauty of Washington's scenery. Both Kizer and Roethke won the Pulitzer Prize for poetry.

▲ Kurt Cobain, one of the most influential musicians of the twentieth century, was born in Hoquiam, Washington. He was the lead singer and guitarist of the band Nirvana.

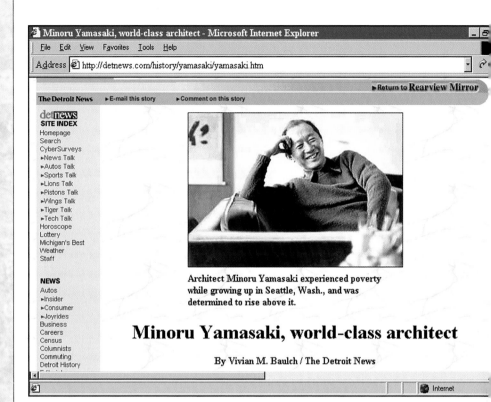

The Detroit News ▶E-mail this story ▶Comment on this story

det**news**
SITE INDEX
Homepage
Search
CyberSurveys
▶News Talk
▶Autos Talk
▶Sports Talk
▶Lions Talk
▶Pistons Talk
▶Wings Talk
▶Tiger Talk
▶Tech Talk
Horoscope
Lottery
Michigan's Best
Weather
Staff

NEWS
Autos
▶Insider
▶Consumer
▶Joyrides
Business
Careers
Census
Columnists
Commuting
Detroit History

Architect Minoru Yamasaki experienced poverty while growing up in Seattle, Wash., and was determined to rise above it.

Minoru Yamasaki, world-class architect

By Vivian M. Baulch / The Detroit News

▲ *World-class architect Minoru Yamasaki was raised in Seattle, Washington. He is well-known for buildings such as the Twin Towers, which collapsed due to a terrorist attack on September 11, 2001.*

Washington novelists include Frank Herbert, creator of the science fiction epic called *Dune*, Ivan Doig, Don Berry, and Ernest K. Gann. Washington artists include painters Robert Motherwell, Mark Tobey, and Jacob Lawrence. Cartoonist Gary Larson, creator of *The Far Side*, was born in Tacoma. An architect from Seattle, Minoru Yamasaki, designed more than three hundred buildings. Unfortunately, his most famous work—New York's World Trade Center—was destroyed in the terrorist attack of September 11, 2001.

Chapter 2 ▶

Land and Climate

Washington is the twentieth-largest state, with an area of 66,582 square miles, not including 1,545 square miles of inland water and 2,511 square miles of coastal water. It is bordered on the north by the Canadian province of British Columbia, on the east by Idaho, on the south by Oregon, and on the west by the Pacific Ocean.

▶ Washington's Five Regions

Washington can be divided into five geographic regions: the Coast Ranges, the Puget Sound Lowland, the Cascade

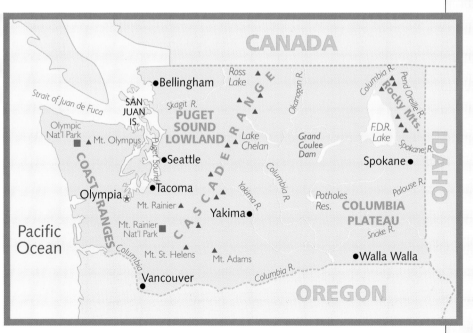

▲ A map of Washington.

Mountains, the Columbia Plateau, and the Rocky Mountains. The Coast Ranges are a chain of mountains that run along Washington's Pacific coast. They are relatively low in southwestern Washington but become taller and more rugged in the Olympic Peninsula, where they are called the Olympic Mountains. The highest mountain in this wilderness region, 7,965-foot Mount Olympus, is covered in snow throughout the year.

Between the Olympic Peninsula and the Cascade Mountains is the Puget Sound Lowland. Puget Sound is a huge body of water, practically enclosed by land on each side. The Strait of Juan de Fuca connects Puget Sound to the Pacific Ocean. About three quarters of Washington's residents live in the cities and towns on the lowland plains bordering Puget Sound. Among the cities are Seattle (the

▲ *The Cascade Mountains separate the western section of the state from the eastern section.*

state's largest city), Tacoma, and Olympia, the state capital. The deep, sheltered waters of the Sound make excellent harbors, and most of Washington's factories and sawmills are located in this region.

East of Puget Sound are the Cascade Mountains, the state's highest mountains. Two of Washington's three national parks—North Cascades and Mount Rainier—are located here. Washington's largest natural lake, Lake Chelan, is at the southern end of North Cascades National Park. The highest Cascade peaks are volcanoes whose upper slopes are covered by glaciers and snow. These include Mount Rainier (14,410 feet), Mount Adams (12,307 feet), and Mount Baker (10,778 feet). There are more than seven hundred glaciers in Washington, more than in any state except Alaska.

Beyond the Cascades are the Rocky Mountains in northeastern Washington. These are separated from the Cascades by the Okanogan River. The Rockies in Washington are a small section of the enormous range that reaches all the way from northern British Columbia in Canada south into Mexico.

To the east of the Rockies lies the Columbia Plateau. This is actually a basin surrounded by higher lands. Much of it is a dry region of sage, grass, and rock. The river valleys of the Yakima, Snake, Wenatchee, and Walla Walla, contain fertile cropland. The southeastern corner of the region, an area of gently rolling hills known as the Palouse country, is a major wheat-growing area. Geological features known as scablands and coulees can be found in an area south and east of a great bend in the Columbia River. Scablands are places where the surface is covered with patches of hard lava rock. Coulees are dry canyons that were carved by water from melting glaciers.

Basalt formations along the Columbia River plateau.

The mighty Columbia River flows south from Canada through the Rocky Mountain region. When it reaches the Columbia Plateau it shifts sharply westward. The massive Grand Coulee Dam, the largest of the eleven major dams along the Columbia in Washington, is located on this stretch of the river. The dam created 150-mile-long Franklin D. Roosevelt Lake, Washington's largest lake. When the Columbia reaches the Cascades, it veers south until it reaches the Oregon border. There it turns to the west and forms the Washington-Oregon border as it flows all the way to the Pacific. The Columbia flows through

Washington for more than 700 miles, making it one of the longest rivers in the United States.

▶ A Region of Fire, Ice, Ash, and Mud

At 8:32 A.M. on May 18, 1980, Mount St. Helens (8,364 feet high) exploded with a mighty roar. This volcano had been quiet for more than one hundred years. Then an earthquake caused a massive landslide of rock, ice, and snow on the mountain. This in turn allowed pressure that had been building inside the volcano to be released in a gigantic eruption. The blast was more powerful than several atomic bombs. The top 1,312 feet of Mount St. Helens (about 8.8 billion cubic yards) were blasted away. A massive plume of ash rose 16 miles into the atmosphere. The blast of heated gas flattened forests for up to 15 miles.

▲ Mount St. Helens erupted violently on May 18, 1980, causing hundreds of millions of dollars in damage to the surrounding area.

Rivers became raging torrents of mud, washing away bridges and homes. Some towns in eastern Washington were coated with up to 7 inches of volcanic ash. Fifty-seven people died as a result of the eruption.

The eruption entirely changed the mountain. "On May 17, 1980, Mount St. Helens was a symmetrical cone, a mountain so near perfection it was sometimes called 'America's Mount Fujiyama.' . . . By the evening of May 18, Mount St. Helens was a smoking crater, hollowed-out and gray. It looked defiled, like the victim of some grisly crime."[1]

▲ *Many scientists worry that Mt. Rainier is overdue for a huge eruption.*

Twenty-one minor eruptions occurred in the next six years, but Mount St. Helens seems to have gone back to sleep. The Mount St. Helens National Volcanic Monument was created in 1982 and has become a major tourist attraction. The surrounding lands are recovering, and plants and animals are returning.

The forces of nature that caused the May 1980 eruption are still at work deep within the earth. Earthquakes and volcanic eruptions will continue to occur in western Washington. On February 28, 2001, Seattle and other parts of the Puget Sound region were rocked by an earthquake that measured 6.8 on the Richter scale. The quake injured more than four hundred people and caused about $3 billion in damage. Scientists worry that Mount Rainier, which has erupted four times in the last four thousand years, may be overdue for a deadly eruption.

▶ Wet and Wetter

Mild west winds from the Pacific Ocean make Washington's winter climate less cold than you would expect for a state so far north. Seattle's average temperature in January is 41°F, which is typical of the Puget Sound region. In summer, these winds have a cooling effect, and provide pleasant temperatures in the 60s. The climate is damp, especially in winter. Most days are gray, and it rains much of the time for eight or nine months of the year. However, much of the time this is just a light drizzle. Seattle receives about 33 inches of rain a year, less than New York City's 41 inches. Occasionally, it is cold enough to snow.

The climate of the Seattle area seems dry compared with parts of the Olympic Peninsula. There, rain clouds moving in from the Pacific brush up against the Olympic

Mountains, resulting in as much as 150 to 200 inches of rain a year. This incredible amount of water is responsible for the rain forests in the river valleys on the west side of the Olympics. East of the Olympics, the San Juan Islands in Puget Sound get relatively little rain, and are said to lie in the "rain shadow" of the Olympics.

The Cascade Mountains receive record snowfalls. Paradise Ranger Station on Mount Rainier recorded 1,122 inches of snow for the winter of 1970–71, a United States record at that time. This record was broken during the winter of 1998–99, when 1,140 inches of snow fell at

▲ *Mount Baker is the northernmost of the Cascade volcanoes in the United States.*

   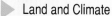

the Mount Baker Ski Area. The Cascades soak up much of the moisture from the clouds. As a result, eastern Washington does not benefit from the moist Pacific air. Eastern Washington is dry, and the winters are colder and summers warmer than in the Puget Sound region.

The Columbia Plateau receives only about 6 inches of rain a year. The city of Spokane has average temperatures of 25°F in January and of 70°F in July. The coldest temperature ever recorded in Washington was −48°F, at Mazama and Winthrop in the northeastern part of the state, on December 30, 1968. The hottest temperature recorded was 118°F, at Ice Harbor Dam in southeastern Washington on August 5, 1961.

Chapter 3

Economy

Washington is rich in natural resources. At one time, all the state's major industries depended on what the land and sea provided.

Coal mining began in the Puget Sound area near Bellingham in the 1850s and in the Cascades in the 1880s.

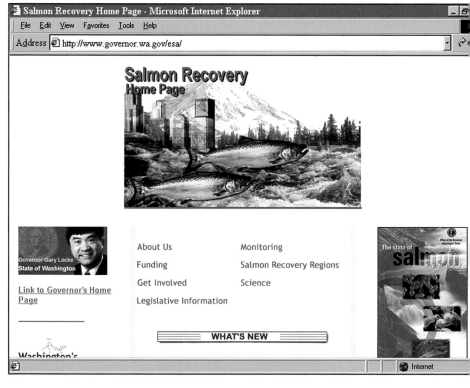

▲ In the past decade, the salmon population off the coast of Washington decreased to alarmingly low levels. In recent years, however, Washington's state government has enacted a salmon recovery plan.

Coal mining had practically disappeared by the 1930s, but today it is making a comeback.

Washington's forests have allowed the state to become one of the nation's leading producers of timber. However, environmental concerns have placed some restrictions on logging recently. In some old-growth forests, logging was stopped entirely to protect an endangered species of bird—the spotted owl. This was good news for the owl, but many loggers lost their jobs.

Fishing, especially for salmon, was always important to Washington's American Indians. Salmon fishing later became a huge industry in the 1860s when canneries were established. However, the number of salmon available recently declined dramatically. There were a number of reasons for this: overfishing, destruction of the salmon's spawning grounds by dams and logging, and a change in ocean currents. Salmon fishing was banned near the coast of Washington until the salmon habitat can be restored. Still, some American Indian tribal fisheries are allowed to continue fishing. Young salmon are now produced in commercial fish hatcheries.

There are more than forty thousand farms in Washington, and more than one third of them are dependent on irrigation for their water supplies. The most valuable field crop is wheat, which is grown in eastern Washington. More apples are grown in Washington than in any other state—about 10 billion apples a year, which explains why the apple is Washington's state fruit.

▶ A Diversified Economy

Washington's economy is much more varied. Industries based on natural resources—farming, mining, lumber, and fishing—are still important. However, less than 10 percent

▲ *Apples remain an important crop to Washington's economy.*

of Washington residents now work in the mining or agricultural industries.

About 60 percent of Washington's workers are employed in service industries—finance, insurance, real estate, computer software, engineering, law, wholesale and retail trade, and various kinds of community, business, and personal services. More than 10 percent work in manufacturing industries such as aerospace, shipbuilding, computer and electronic products, telecommunications equipment, and medical equipment. About 15 percent work for the federal, state, and local governments. Others work in transportation, communication, utilities, and construction.

Many of Washington's most successful corporations are in or near Seattle. Microsoft, headquartered in Redmond, is the world's biggest producer of software. Boeing, one of the world's largest manufacturers of airplanes and spacecraft, has major manufacturing facilities in Seattle. Other well-known companies based in Seattle are Amazon.com, Nordstrom, Eddie Bauer, Inc., Washington Mutual Savings, and Starbucks. Weyerhaeuser, which makes wood and paper products, is headquartered in Tacoma.

Seattle and Tacoma are major ports and are important in trade with Asia. They handle shipping containers, the large cargo boxes carried by ocean-going freighters. Two major transportation companies based in Seattle are Alaska Air Group and Airborne Freight.

▶ Water, Water Everywhere

Washington has nearly eight thousand lakes and reservoirs. So it is not surprising that more than 80 percent of

▲ Although many large corporations are based in Washington, farming still plays an important role in the state's economy.

▲ *The Diablo Dam on the Upper Skagit River is just one of Washington's many dams.*

the state's energy comes from hydroelectricity. Dams were built on various rivers to provide electric power. The Bonneville Dam on the Columbia River was completed in 1938. The Grand Coulee Dam—also on the Columbia and completed in 1941—is the largest concrete dam in the world and one of the world's greatest sources of hydro-electric power. In addition to providing electric power, the dams provide water to irrigate the land in much of central Washington.

▶ Why the Tourists Keep Coming

Washington offers spectacular sights, awesome scenery, and a wide variety of activities from relaxing cruises on the water, to hiking and camping, climbing, and winter sports. Even in July, skiing is possible in the Cascades—at Mount

Baker and other places. If you are really adventurous, a helicopter will fly you to remote slopes. There is lots of boating on Washington's waters, and white-water kayaking is especially exciting on rivers in the Cascades. If you just want to watch sports, teams include the Seahawks (football), the SuperSonics (basketball), the Thunderbirds (minor-league ice hockey), and the Mariners (baseball).

Seattle, often called the "Emerald City," is a major tourist attraction with music, ballet, art, theater, and museums. Its hills and long waterfront make it a wonderful city for walking. A monorail—the nation's first—links downtown Seattle with the Space Needle and its wonderful views.

One of the most fascinating places is the Pike Place Market, where you can buy everything from fresh fish to handicrafts. The city is also known for its beautiful glass objects. Only Venice, Italy, has more glassblowers living and working there.

▲ A view of Seattle at night.

Chapter 4

Government

On November 11, 1889, Washington became the forty-second state in the Union. Washington might have been named Columbia, after the mighty river. Federal officials were afraid this might be mistaken for the nation's capital—the District of Columbia.

So it was named Washington instead. Of course, now there are two Washingtons that can be confused.

▶ Washington's Constitution

Washington's constitution was adopted in 1889. It outlines the structure of the state government and describes the powers of its branches and departments. Women were not allowed to vote in Washington at first. In 1909, the state legislature approved an amendment that changed this. In 1910, the amendment was approved by the voters.

▶ The Structure of Washington's Government

Like the federal government, Washington's government is divided into three branches—executive, legislative, and judicial. The chief executive is the governor, who is elected by the voters to a four-year term. The governor's job is to uphold the laws.

The legislative branch is made up of a 49-member senate and a 98-member house of representatives. Senators serve four-year terms and representatives serve two-year terms. The legislators' main job is to propose new laws.

The judicial branch consists of the court system. The courts interpret the law. The highest court in the state is the state supreme court.

There are also county, city, and town governments. In 1948, counties were given the power to choose their own form of government. The constitution also allows cities with more than twenty thousand residents to have home rule, or the power to choose their own system of local government. Ten of Washington's nearly three hundred incorporated cities and towns have home rule.

Women have played an important role in the state government. Two women were elected to the state legislature

▲ Gary Locke was elected governor of Washington in 1996, making him the first Chinese-American governor in United States history.

in 1912. By 1999, 40 percent of Washington's legislators were women. Dixy Lee Ray, a biologist who had previously headed the U.S. Atomic Energy Commission, became Washington's first woman governor. She served from 1977 to 1981. After retiring to her home, she wrote two books about the environment. They are called *Environmental Overkill* and *Trashing the Planet.*

Chapter 5

History

Many thousands of years ago, during the last Ice Age, the sea level was much lower than it is today. A land bridge connected Alaska and Siberia, and much of North America was covered by glaciers. Perhaps as early as forty thousand years ago, the first people began migrating to North America from Asia. They were nomadic hunters and followed herds of wild animals across the land bridge. About twelve thousand years ago, the first groups of people entered what is now the state of Washington.

▶ The Earliest Washingtonians

The first inhabitants of Washington, the ancestors of today's American Indians, were descendants of the people from Asia. Many groups of American Indians lived in present-day Washington. Coastal tribes—such as the Chinook, Makah, Nooksack, Snoqualmie, Snohomish, and Nisqually—lived west of the Cascades, along the shores of Puget Sound and on the Olympic Peninsula. They used canoes carved from the trunks of large cedar trees. They fished for salmon in the rivers. Some native people, such as the Makah, also hunted whales in the Pacific Ocean using huge seagoing canoes and wooden harpoons.

The Coastal Indians are famous for their traditional ceremony known as the "potlatch." The potlatch was held to celebrate important tribal events such as a birth, death, or marriage. A wealthy family would host the potlatch and would give away its possessions during the ceremony. The

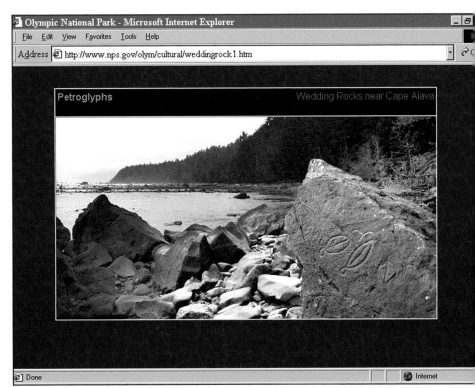

Address http://www.nps.gov/olym/cultural/weddingrock1.htm

Petroglyphs   Wedding Rocks near Cape Alava

▲ *Petroglyphs, or images carved in rock, were likely created by Washington's early inhabitants.*

guests, who included American Indians from other tribes, were expected to do the same at a future potlatch.

Plateau Indians—including such groups as the Nez Percé, Yakima, Cayuse, and Palouse—lived east of the Cascades. In contrast to the Coastal Indians, who lived in established villages, the Plateau Indians kept the nomadic lifestyle of their ancient ancestors. Living conditions were more difficult east of the Cascades, and the Plateau Indians had to move around in search of food and shelter.

The Coastal and Plateau Indians lived undisturbed for thousands of years. Then, in 1592, a Greek explorer using the Spanish name Juan de Fuca, sailed up the coast

of Washington. As in other parts of America, the arrival of the Europeans would change life for the American Indians living in the Northwest.

Explorers, Traders, and Settlers

During the 1700s, Russian, Spanish, English, and American ships sailed along the Washington coast. In 1775, a Spanish expedition led by Bruno de Heceta and Juan Francisco de Bodega y Quadra reached the coast of the Olympic Peninsula. Heceta claimed the land for Spain. At the Spaniards' next stop, the first meeting between Europeans and American Indians ended in tragedy. Seven men who were sent ashore for wood and water were killed by natives.

A number of explorers followed, some with well-known names such as the English explorer Captain James Cook who sailed along the coast in 1776. In 1792, the American Robert Gray reached the mouth of a wide river and named it the Columbia after his ship. That same year, an English captain called George Vancouver explored Puget Sound and named it after one of his officers. He also named several of the mountains in the Cascades after his officers, including Rainier and Baker.

The early explorers traded with the natives. Many more Europeans and Americans followed when they learned of the fine furs that were available. France had acquired much of the land west of the Mississippi River from Spain in 1800. Three years later, the United States acquired the territory from France in the Louisiana Purchase. In 1804, Meriwether Lewis and William Clark led an expedition west to explore America's new lands. With the help of their guide, Sacajawea, a Shoshone Indian woman, Lewis and Clark crossed the Rocky Mountains.

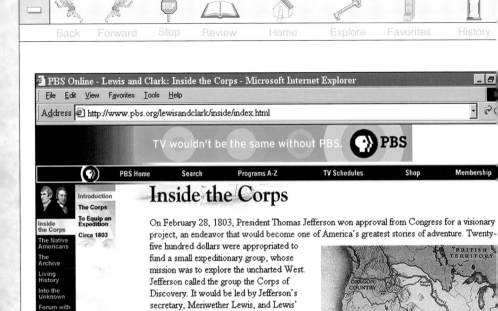

PBS Online - Lewis and Clark: Inside the Corps - Microsoft Internet Explorer

File   Edit   View   Favorites   Tools   Help

Address http://www.pbs.org/lewisandclark/inside/index.html

TV wouldn't be the same without PBS.   PBS

PBS Home   Search   Programs A-Z   TV Schedules   Shop   Membership

Introduction
The Corps
To Equip an
Expedition
Circa 1803

Inside
the Corps
The Native
Americans
The
Archive
Living
History
Into the
Unknown
Forum with
Ken Burns
Classroom
Resources
Related
Products

online   GM

Inside the Corps

On February 28, 1803, President Thomas Jefferson won approval from Congress for a visionary project, an endeavor that would become one of America's greatest stories of adventure. Twenty-five hundred dollars were appropriated to fund a small expeditionary group, whose mission was to explore the uncharted West. Jefferson called the group the Corps of Discovery. It would be led by Jefferson's secretary, Meriwether Lewis, and Lewis' friend, William Clark.

Over the next four years, the Corps of Discovery would travel thousands of miles, experiencing lands, rivers and peoples that no Americans ever had before.

Inside the Corps has three sections: Circa 1803, To Equip an Expedition and the Corps.

Lewis and Clark's Outbound Route Shown in Red, Inbound in Blue

Internet

Lewis and Clark traveled along the Columbia River and reached the West Coast on November 15, 1805.

When they reached the Columbia River, they traveled by canoe. The river took them all the way to the Pacific Coast. They arrived at the mouth of the Columbia on November 15, 1805.

In the following years, fur traders established trading posts in a vast area that came to be called the Oregon Country. It included present-day Oregon, Washington, Idaho, Montana, and the southern part of British Columbia, including Vancouver Island. Trading companies included the North West Company and the Hudson's Bay Company (both British Canadian) and the Pacific Fur

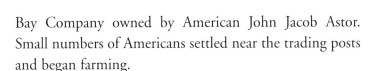

Bay Company owned by American John Jacob Astor. Small numbers of Americans settled near the trading posts and began farming.

During these years, England and the United States both claimed the Oregon Country. In 1815, the Treaty of Ghent, which ended the War of 1812 between England and the United States, gave both countries the right to the region for a period of ten years. The ten-year agreement was renewed twice, and the official northern border of the United States was set at the 49th parallel in a final compromise in 1846.

Meanwhile, the Organic Act of 1843 granted a 640-acre parcel of free land to any white American male who could mark its boundaries, file a claim, and build a cabin on it. That year, about nine hundred settlers traveled to the Oregon Country in what was known as the "Great Migration." Unfortunately for the American Indians, the whites were legally entitled to take away their land. As more and more whites moved into the area, tensions grew between the native peoples and the settlers.

By 1848, many settlers were living in the Oregon Country. President James K. Polk then created the Oregon Territory. To get there, most of the settlers traveled along the Oregon Trail from St. Joseph, Missouri. In 1853, the Washington Territory was separated from the Oregon Territory. At the time, Washington had a population of less than four thousand. By 1880, the population had grown to more than 125,000. Towns had grown at the main areas of settlement, such as Seattle and Olympia west of the Cascades, and Spokane and Walla Walla in eastern Washington.

As Washington's white population increased, the American Indians lost more and more of their traditional

lands. Washington Territory's first governor, Isaac I. Stevens, set out to push the native peoples off their land. Many Coastal Indian tribes had to sign treaties giving up their lands. In the process, more than seventeen thousand Indians were forced onto reservations. In 1855, Chief Sealth, a Salish Indian living on Bainbridge Island, signed a treaty giving all the land around Puget Sound to the United States. In a speech at the time, Sealth mourned the sad fate of the American Indians and the loss of their lands and way of life:

> When the last Red Man shall have perished, and the memory of my tribe shall have become a myth among the white man, these shores will swarm with the invisible dead of my tribe . . . At night when the streets of your cities are silent and you think them deserted, they will throng with the returning hosts that once filled them and still love this beautiful land . . .[1]

David Maynard, a friend of Chief Sealth, changed the name of the town of Duwamps to Seattle, in honor of the chief. White settlers pronounced Sealth's name "See-at-el." Meanwhile, some Plateau Indian tribes in eastern Washington decided to fight for their lands and refused to sign treaties. The three-year-long Yakima Indian War ended in 1858 when the coalition of local tribes was defeated by United States soldiers at the Battle of Four Lakes.

The Growth of a Modern State

By 1889, the year that Washington became a state, the population had grown to 357,000. Busy sawmills around Puget Sound shipped lumber to California and as far away as Australia and eastern Asia. Towns near sawmills grew into cities. The Northern Pacific Railroad, which connected Washington with the East Coast, was completed in 1883.

The railroads brought many new residents to Washington and stimulated the growth of industry. Spokane became an important rail hub and grew rapidly. Seattle became a major base for shipping supplies to the prospectors in the Klondike gold rush of 1897–98.

The Alaska-Yukon-Pacific Exposition drew nearly 4 million visitors to Seattle in 1909. The huge fair showed the world that the city had become a center of culture and commerce. By 1910, more than a million people lived in Washington. The building of dams on Washington's rivers not only provided hydroelectric power for homes and factories, but also made farming possible on a large scale.

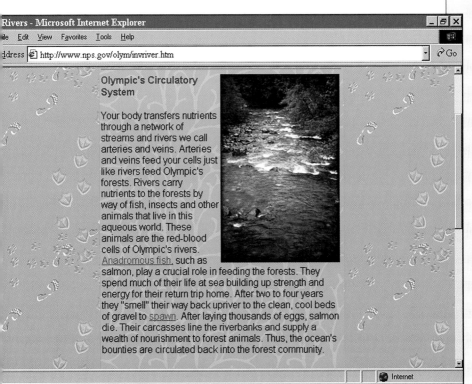

Rivers - Microsoft Internet Explorer

File   Edit   View   Favorites   Tools   Help

Address http://www.nps.gov/olym/invriver.htm   Go

Olympic's Circulatory System

Your body transfers nutrients through a network of streams and rivers we call arteries and veins. Arteries and veins feed your cells just like rivers feed Olympic's forests. Rivers carry nutrients to the forests by way of fish, insects and other animals that live in this aqueous world. These animals are the red-blood cells of Olympic's rivers. Anadromous fish, such as salmon, play a crucial role in feeding the forests. They spend much of their life at sea building up strength and energy for their return trip home. After two to four years they "smell" their way back upriver to the clean, cool beds of gravel to spawn. After laying thousands of eggs, salmon die. Their carcasses line the riverbanks and supply a wealth of nourishment to forest animals. Thus, the ocean's bounties are circulated back into the forest community.

▲ *Washingtonians are concerned with protecting their state's natural environment. Special efforts have been made to prevent further pollution of the rivers.*

Indeed, by 1910, the whole Yakima region consisted of irrigated farmland. In 1917, Washington's economy—especially shipbuilding and forest and agricultural products—boomed after the United States entered World War I.

During the Great Depression of the 1930s, unemployment was widespread. However, the food processing industry remained healthy throughout those years. The building of Bonneville and Grand Coulee dams in the late 1930s helped turn the state's economy around. During World War II in the 1940s, defense-related industries prospered in Washington. The Boeing Company in Seattle built the B-17 bomber and employed more than fifty thousand workers. Washington's aluminum plants produced half the nation's supply of that metal.

While Washington's economy experienced dynamic growth during the war years, this was a sad and difficult time for Washingtonians of Japanese descent. President Franklin D. Roosevelt had them sent to internment camps for the duration of the war.

In 1962, the Seattle World's Fair, known as Century 21, drew millions of visitors and helped to stimulate growth of the state's tourism industry.

▶ Washington Today

Today Washingtonians are faced with exciting opportunities and daunting challenges. New companies in areas such as biotechnology and computer software continue to provide exciting job opportunities. This, combined with the state's scenery and recreational advantages, continues to draw new residents. How can the state continue to grow and yet remain desirable? Seattle has often been called one of the nation's "most livable" cities in national magazines.[2]

▲ *Efforts have been made to help clean up the Columbia River.*

Preserving Washington's beautiful environment for future generations has become an urgent concern. An especially critical situation exists at Hanford in southeastern Washington. In 1943, during World War II, the government built the Hanford Works, a nuclear energy center. Hanford workers contributed to the creation of the first atomic bombs. Unfortunately, in recent years, radioactive liquid nuclear waste has leaked from underground tanks at Hanford and has polluted the Columbia River. A major cleanup effort is now underway. Determined to protect their environment, Washingtonians can look forward to a bright future.

Chapter 1. The Evergreen State

1. Ruth Kirk, *The Olympic Rain Forest* (Seattle: University of Washington Press, 1966), p. 5.

Chapter 2. Land and Climate

1. Rob Carson, *Mount St. Helens: The Eruption and Recovery of a Volcano* (Seattle: Sasquatch Books, 1990), p. 9.

Chapter 5. History

1. Chief Sealth, as quoted in Carolyn Kizer, *Proses: On Poems and Poets* (Port Townsend, Wash.: Copper Canyon Press, 1993), p. 98.

2. "Demographics: King County Overview," *Economic Development Council of Seattle and King County*, 2001–02, <http://www.edc-sea.org/research_data/economic_demographics.cfm> (August 30, 2002).

Further Reading

Blashfield, Jean F. *Washington.* Danbury, Conn.: Children's Press, 2001.

Bredeson, Carmen. *Mount St. Helens Volcano: Violent Eruption.* Berkeley Heights, N.J.: Enslow Publishers, Inc., 2001.

Cocke, William: *A Historical Album of Washington.* Brookfield, Conn.: The Millbrook Press, 1995.

Colasurdo, Christine. *Return to Spirit Lake: Journey Through a Lost Landscape.* Seattle: Sasquatch Books, 1997.

Furtwangler, Albert. *Answering Chief Seattle.* Seattle: University of Washington Press, 1997.

Kavanagh, James. *Washington Wildlife.* Blaine, Wash.: Waterford Press, 1997.

Kirk, Ruth and Carmela Alexander. *Exploring Washington's Past: A Road Guide to History.* Seattle: University of Washington Press, 1990.

Pitcher, Don: *Washington Handbook.* Chico, Calif.: Moon Publications, 1999.

Strudwick, Leslie. *A Guide to Washington.* Mankato, Minn.: Weigl Publishers, Inc., 2001.

Womack, Randy L. *Washington Geography.* Redding, Calif.: Golden Educational Center, 1998.

Index